A Sketchbook of Birds

C. F. Tunnicliffe R.A.
A Sketchbook of Birds

Introduction by Ian Niall

LONDON
VICTOR GOLLANCZ LTD
1979

Introduction © Ian Niall 1979
Illustrations © Mrs Dorothy Downes 1979

First published July 1979
Second impression July 1979

ISBN 0 575 02640 5

Printed in Italy by
A. Mondadori Editore, Verona

Contents

Publisher's Note

The sketches reproduced in this book are taken from seventeen sketchbooks filled by the artist between 1934 and 1962. Some of the larger sketches have been slightly reduced in order to fit the page.

Most of the sketches were made at two locations: the island of Anglesey, where Charles Tunnicliffe lived from 1947 until his death in February 1979, and the country near Macclesfield in Cheshire, where he spent the first twenty-odd years of his life, and frequently re-visited.

In nearly all cases, Tunnicliffe noted on his sketches the location and the date of composition; the year of composition and the scientific names of the birds have been added in the captions.

The publisher acknowledges with gratitude the unfailing assistance of the artist's sister, Mrs Dorothy Downes, and of Mr and Mrs Ian Niall, without whom the book could not have been published.

Sadly, Charles Tunnicliffe did not live to see publication of this book, but he saw colour proofs of some of the pictures and took pleasure in discussing and corresponding about publishing details during the planning stages. His last letter, giving details of his early wood-engravings, was received at the Gollancz office on the day of his death.

Introduction
by Ian Niall

In popular imagination a romantic aura surrounds the lives of artists, but I have always believed that any artist who is more than a nine days' wonder must have an essentially practical approach. Great talent is cultivated in interminable days, in years of striving to master a technique, in applying continually a special imagination, which is the artist's gift.

Charles Tunnicliffe, the son of ordinary farming folk from Cheshire, was a man whose application, whose undaunted perseverance, put my own rather superficial approach to most things in shameful shade.

I first knew of him (in common with thousands of others) as the illustrator of Henry Williamson's famous books *Tarka the Otter* (1932) and *Salar the Salmon* (1935). Before this, Tunnicliffe had sold some superb etchings while still a student at the Royal College of Art. Most went into private collections, but some were purchased by the Victoria and Albert Museum in London and the National Gallery, Stockholm. He was quickly making his name as an engraver and illustrator of the first rank, and his work for Williamson was the prelude to a lifetime of illustrating books for authors small and great (Hemingway, Negley Farson, H. E. Bates and Richard Church among them). To all of these, and to many others, Tunnicliffe brought something exceptional, an uncanny sensitivity, the ability to enter the author's fantasy – the mark of the great illustrator.

Twelve or thirteen years ago I met Charles Tunnicliffe for the first time. His home on the island of Anglesey was not far from mine above Llandudno in North Wales. We began to correspond, and to meet from time to time and I formed the idea that I might one day write about his life and art. Although I am neither an ornithologist nor a student of art, I felt that I might bring a certain understanding to the task. We came from similar backgrounds. Eventually I decided to put away other work and prepare a biography. Charles greeted my proposal diffidently (being the most modest of men) but agreed to see me each week. We talked about his early life in Macclesfield, his struggles to make a living as an artist, his marriage, his experiences with the highly inflammable Henry Williamson. Throughout, he would punctuate any reminiscence with amazingly wide ranging observations on birds and animals. For me, our meetings were far more than nostalgia; I was sitting at the feet of a great naturalist and a great observer. Charles had studied birds with an artist's, not a shooting man's, eye. He knew the golden plover's flight, the juvenile plumage of the rare northern variety, the feeding rituals of falcons and cormorants, the precise extent of a snowy owl's wing. This vast knowledge was recorded in his field notes and sketchbooks, an amazing collection of the most detailed study and the finest art in themselves.

As the pages of my notes increased, I felt that it was time to look for a publisher. My friend and fishing companion, David Burnett of Victor Gollancz, needed no second invitation to come up from London and talk about the book with Charles and myself. When he arrived at my house I proceeded to talk him into the ground about *The Life and Art of Charles Tunnicliffe*. On the journey over to Anglesey he kept falling asleep as I continued at length to describe the marvels that Tunnicliffe had shown me, including his drawings for the original wood-engravings for *Tarka*, and his extraordinary 'bird maps', large scale detailed studies of hundreds of birds, some of which I thought might go into my book. On arriving at Shorelands, the house at Malltraeth where Tunnicliffe lived for thirty years, we looked together at the 'bird maps' and then I once again took up with Charles the thread of our previous discussion. My publishing friend had fallen into a kind of reverie over some sketchbooks he had found casually stowed in a cupboard. It seemed to me that he was pondering technical problems. I was afraid that he would say that my book could not be illustrated in the generous way I had hoped. Suddenly he remarked that here was treasure trove. Tunnicliffe's bird sketches were something the world must see. There was nothing like them. They called for the finest possible reproduction, paper and printing. Everyone who loved beautiful work would want to possess a book of the sketches, as a boy wants to keep the exotic butterfly he cups in his hands. Bird-watchers, ornithologists and artists would all be enchanted by it. Tunnicliffe blinked for a moment and smiled at this enthusiasm. In a long life dedicated to his art he had accumulated so much work of such breath-taking quality that he thought no more about it, but we were thinking about it and the need to let the world see it. Would he entrust the priceless sketchbooks to the publisher's care for a while so that the pictures could be photographed? Tunnicliffe had a generous nature and he graciously agreed. And so *A Sketchbook of Birds* was born.

Tunnicliffe's *alter ego* was art. In the face of this unturnable force, his parents accepted that their son must be allowed to cultivate his talent and could not remain to help them on the farm. He went, first by one scholarship to Macclesfield School of Art and then by another to the Royal College of Art. From there he proceeded to exhibit at and then to be admitted to the Royal Academy. In 1977, towards the end of a great career, his name appeared in the Queen's Birthday Honours List. Along the way, and in the course of the busiest lifetime any artist can ever have had, he amassed sketches – some of the best of which are published here. Charles Tunnicliffe's *Sketchbook of Birds* speaks for itself. Writing an introduction to it, I know that my words will be read not before but after the reader has turned the pages in wonder, over and over again.

Tunnicliffe's place in art is assured by virtue of endless work at the easel and drawing board. My problem is to find words to put upon it – obsession, perfectionism, meticulous care, beauty. I remember Charles once quoting me the favourite tag of one of his professors at the Royal Academy one day when we were talking about the nature of art – 'Tell me where is fancy bred, or in the heart or in the head?' There is no answer, but fancy – the conception of beauty – being there, Tunnicliffe fostered it when he could, to the exclusion of everything else, and for a life-time. People will go on collecting Tunnicliffe's prints, coveting those early etchings – *The Bull*, *The Cheshire Plain*, *A Winter Landscape* – coveting also the water-colours snatched up by eager buyers on the first day of the Academy exhibitions, long after most of his contemporaries are forgotten. If I commented further on the *Sketchbook of Birds* it would be to remind those who have seen it that they are enjoying a very privileged view of the quiet life of a private man – and a great artist.

Tan-yr-Allt Cottage
Llandudno, February 1979

Location Notes to the Sketches

The purpose of these brief notes is to enable the reader to locate on a map the sites referred to in Tunnicliffe's sketches. In a few cases, identification of the sites is uncertain. Most sites are either close to Macclesfield, the artist's home town in Cheshire, or on the island of Anglesey, where he made his home in 1947 and where he remained until his death.

Alderley Edge—Cheshire. To the north-west of Macclesfield.

Amlwch—ancient port in north Anglesey.

Anglesey—island situated off the north coast of Wales. First connected to the mainland by Thomas Telford's famous bridge across the Menai Strait.

Beaumaris—Anglesey, at the eastern end of the Menai Strait.

Birtles Pool—west of Macclesfield, in the grounds of Birtles Hall.

Bodorgan headland—south-west Anglesey, north of the Cefni estuary.

Bont Farm—near the artist's home, south-west Anglesey.

Bosley Reservoir—south of Macclesfield, by the A54 and A523 road junction.

Capesthorne Pool—west of Macclesfield in the grounds of Capesthorne Hall.

Cemlyn Lake—on the north coast of Anglesey, west of Amlwch.

Clitheroe—(Bradley Hall) Lancashire.

Clough Brook—a stream near the artist's birthplace, south of Macclesfield.

Cob Lake—by Malltraeth, Anglesey.

Crochan Caffo—a pool in the marshes near Llangaffo, Anglesey.

Dinas Point—by Bodorgan, off the northern shore of the Cefni estuary.

Foel Ferry—near the western end of the Menai Strait on the Anglesey side, opposite Caernarvon (the ferry no longer operates).

Foryd Estuary—North Wales, across the Menai Strait from Anglesey, at the western end.

Gawsworth Pool—south of Macclesfield in the grounds of Gawsworth Hall.

Glan Avon—probably Glanrafon, a farm near the artist's home in Anglesey.

Goldsitch Moss—country area to the south-east of Macclesfield.

Gull Island, Aberdaron—off the coast of north-west Wales. The two islands are usually called 'The Gwyllans'.

Handa Island, Sutherland—Scotland, off the north-west highland coast.

Hawk's-head Clough—near Higher Sutton, Macclesfield.

Iona—island off the south-west shore of Mull, north-west Scotland.

Kendal—south-west Lake District, Westmorland.

Llandwyn lighthouse—Llandwyn Island, south Anglesey, on the southern side of the Cefni estuary.

Lligwy Bay—on the north-east coast of Anglesey.

Llyn Coron—a small lake near Bodorgan railway station, south-west Anglesey.

Macclesfield—Cheshire. The artist's home town, just north of Langley, his birthplace.

Malltraeth Lake—near the artist's home, south-west Anglesey.

Moelfre—on the north-east coast of Anglesey.

Nant Bychan rocks—north-east coast of Anglesey, between Traeth Bychan and Moelfre.

Northwich—Cheshire. A small town to the west of Macclesfield.

Pont Aber Glaslyn—Snowdonia, North Wales, in the mountain pass south of Beddgelert (A498 road).

Porth Aber (usually Porth yr Aber)—near Moelfre on the east coast of Anglesey.

Radnor Mere—a lake south of Nether Alderley, to the north-west of Macclesfield.

Radnor Woods—beech woods south of Nether Alderley, to the north-west of Macclesfield.

Redesmere—a lake west of Macclesfield, Cheshire.

Shorelands—the artist's home by Malltraeth, south-west Anglesey.

South Stack—cliffs off the north-west coast of Holy Island, Anglesey.

Stack Rocks—A group of rocks in St Bride's Bay to the north-east of Skomer Island. In 1938 CFT and his wife were marooned on the island by bad weather for some days and were forced to live off seagull's eggs.

Traeth Bach—estuary in north-west Wales, south of Porthmadog.

Traeth Bychan—a small bay on the north-east coast of Anglesey, south of Moelfre.

Ty Gwyn—south of Cefni Reservoir, Llangefni, Anglesey.

Y Felin—literally 'The Mill', of which there are several near the artist's home on Anglesey. The precise location is unknown.

Seabirds

1 Common gull, *Larus canus*, on the island of Iona, Argyll, September 1934.
2 Great black-backed gull, *Larus marinus*, Iona, September 25th, 1934.
3 Young herring gull, *Larus argentatus*, Iona, September 1934.

Iona Sept. 25ᵗʰ
Gr Black-backed gull.

Seen singly. Sometimes with
a crowd of common gulls resting
on the machair. Today seen
feeding on the body of a dead
dog & thrown up at White Sands
bay. Two Hoody crows also feeding
with him.
Seen also in the pastures
behind the farms on rising
ground resting with a young
gull.
In Iona regarded as the king
of thieves and murderers.

"From memory."

From life.

2

Young Herring gull.

Iona. Sept.

3

4 Studies of immature herring gull, *Larus argentatus*, Moelfre, September 1944.

Stream running through.
shingle beach south of Beaumaris.
Two plumages of Juvenile Black-headed Gull
the sitting bird was pale and browner on scapulars
and wings and had no brown suffusion on sides of
breast and flanks. Amount of colour on heads varies
also

July 13th

5

5 Juvenile black-headed gulls, *Larus ridibundus,* near Beaumaris, July 13th, probably 1948.

June 13th ... Black ...

Scapulars darker grey than
... coverts.
Slight collar.

Tail pale grey
and grey white tips.
Legs grey & feet.

Beak amber green
and yellowish.
towards the tip.
Tube blackish

6 Fulmar, *Fulmarus glacialis*, near Stack Rock. June 13th, 1938.
7 Shags, *Phalacrocorax aristotelis:* adult with young, and juvenile. Bodorgan headland, May 1948.

8

8 Cormorant, *Phalacrocorax carbo*, nestling, Bodorgan headland, July 17th, 1949.
9 Puffins, *Fratercula arctica*, Gull Island, Aberdaron, July 30th, 1935.

Just before landing

(1)

(2)

(3)

July 30th. Gull Island, Abrawon
Puffins still taking fish to their nesting burrows

Lands with feet extended as above
then falls rather clumsily forward on
its breast causing a splash.

skin round the eye
leaden grey blue

9

June 2nd
Common Terns. Nant Bychan
Rock.
One preening on a rock. Other
brought a fish to it but preening
bird ignored it and flew away.
Other bird at once swallowed fish

10 Common terns, *Sterna hirundo*, one offering a fish. Nant Bychan rocks, June 2nd, 1942.

June 3rd Lligwy Bay.
Pair of Little Terns. Suspect they
are the same pair noted at Traeth
Bychan as they were at Lligwy
during high tide when all the sand
at Traeth Bychan is covered.

Slight display and calling before flying off, after a stay with its mate

11

11 Pair of little terns, *Sterna albifrons*, Lligwy Bay, June 3rd, 1942.

These two Oystercatchers stayed on
rock till a wave became too big
& threatening. Incoming tide
April 28th. Rocks near Traeth Bychan

12 Oystercatchers, *Haematopus ostralegus*, on the rocks near Traeth Bychan, April 28th, 1946.

Two Great Black-backs swimming
at the edge of the weed. One holding
wings *outside* flank feathers.

13 Pair of great black-backed gulls, *Larus marinus*, 1944 or 1945.

may 19th Malltraeth
Lake.

Little Terns feeding from the
lake and would rest in
groups on the mud in company
with Dunlin and Common
Terns.

14

14 Little terns, *Sterna albifrons*, feeding and resting, Malltraeth Lake, May 19th, 1945.

15

15 Autumn sandwich terns, *Sterna sandvicensis*, and one common tern, Lligwy Bay,
September 8th, 1944.

16 Oystercatchers, *Haematopus ostralegus*, ringed plover, *Charadrius hiaticula*, and a teal, *Anas crecca*, Nant Bychan rocks, evening, September 10th, 1944.

Inside of legs dusty yellow ochre

Oct 2nd. Probably Juvenile Guillemot changing to 1st winter.

17 Juvenile guillemot, *Uria aalge,* changing to first winter plumage, October 2nd, 1948.

18

18 Razorbill, *Alca torda*, in winter plumage, probably autumn 1947.
19 Guillemots, *Uria aalge*, Handa Island, Sutherland, June 16th, 1939.

Guillemots.   Handa Island June 16"
3 sitting together in a sheltered corner of rock exposed
to the sun. Much neck stretching and peering as I drew
them

Yellow   Sepia Brown   Black

19

Rocks above Porth Aber.

Common Tern. Rested on the edge of a
flat shelf of rock on which we were also
resting. Clayton watched for almost one minute
not more than six yards away.

20 Common tern, *Sterna hirundo,* on rocks above Porth Aber, June 1942.

21 Common terns, *Sterna hirundo*, one presenting a fish, Amlwch, June 1942.

June 2nd Amlwch Rocks
(Opposite Amlwch Island on which were
many Terns)

Common Terns. Facing a high wind. They often
spread their tails to preserve balance.

On the slopes of Amlwch Island they squatted close and looked like a mass of
fowl-grey eggs.

22

22 Common terns, *Sterna hirundo*, facing a high wind, Amlwch, June 2nd, 1942.
23 Studies of guillemots, *Uria aalge*, Stack Rock, June 12th, 1938.

Black-heads. Traeth Bychan. Sept 4th.
One with a very pronounced rosy breast an
undersides. Others with less noticeable rosy tinge

Traces of the blackish
hood still to be seen in
this bird.

From memory

24

24 Autumn black-headed gulls, *Larus ridibundus*, and an immature herring gull, *Larus argentatus*, Traeth Bychan, September 4th, 1944.
25 Black-headed gulls, *Larus ridibundus*, swimming, Iona, September 19th, 1934.

"Black Headed Gull.
Sept. 19th IONA.

25

June 5. Nant Bychan
Rocks

Turnstones. Small flock of 8 or 9
one very fine cock bird among them.
Plumage of the others very varied
and confusing.

26 Turnstones, *Arenaria interpres*, at Nant Bychan rocks, June 5th, 1942.

Little Tern June 3rd 42
Traeth Bychan.
again being fed by its mate which
on one occasion brought a bigger fish
than usual which the other bird at first
refused to touch. The bird eventually persuaded
her to take it but had to kill the struggling fish before she would do so.

Lit by its evening sun. Looked very yellow.

27 Little tern, *Sterna albifrons*, in evening sunlight, Traeth Bychan, June 3rd, 1942.

Nant Bychan Rocks.
Small party of Turnstones hunted the sea-rocks
during our stay. among them one very fine adult ♂ bird

28

28 Turnstones, *Arenaria interpres*, at Nant Bychan rocks, June 1942.

29 Oystercatchers, *Haematopus ostralegus,* at Nant Bychan rocks, June 4th, 1942.

30 Black-headed gulls, *Larus ridibundus*, showing variation in first summer plumage,
Malltraeth Lake, June 2nd, 1944.

Waders

31 Wood sandpiper, *Tringa glareola*, probably a juvenile, Cob Lake, August 20th, 1952.

august 20th. Ert Lake.
Wood Sandpiper. Probably a juvenile.

Oct. 5' *Grey Plover* on shore in front of the house . . 1 in the morning
Feeding on worms   4 in the evening

also seen up to Oct 15ᵗʰ on the shore

32 Grey plover, *Pluvialis squatarola*, on the shore at Malltraeth, October 5th, 1950.

Curlew Sandpiper. Malltraeth Lake
First week in September. Usually with
Dunlin but occasionally in a flock
exclusively of C. Samples.

33

33 Curlew sandpiper, *Calidris ferruginea*, Malltraeth Lake, September 1945.
34 Knot, *Calidris canutus*, feeding at Cob Lake, September 12th, 1952.
35 The same three knot, four days later.

Sept 12: Bob Lake. 9 Knot feeding in
the mud into rapid probs - 4 per second. With them
4 Curlew Sandpiper, near Dunlin and one Bl.T. Godwit.

34

Sept. 16th. 3 Knots on Pett Lake, still.
also 1 Bar.T. Godwit 6 Bt. Godwit. Many Dunlin.
3 Little Stints. 1 Greenshank. Herons Swans Gulls
(black headed) Oyster catchers, Cormorant,
no Curlew Sandpiper Terns.

Aug 2nd. Young Lapwing. N.B. Under tail coverts curling up above tail.

36 Studies of juvenile lapwing, *Vanellus vanellus*, August 2nd, 1948.

In some birds this pale margin to the mantle very noticeable.

May 18th Dunlin on the mud of Cob Lake.

37

37 Dunlin, *Calidris alpina*, in breeding plumage at Cob Lake, May 18th, 1949.

38 Solitary ruff, *Philomachus pugnax,* at Malltraeth Lake, September 9th, 1946.

Sept 8th Lligwy Beach.
Juvenile Sanderlings in a flock
of fifteen feeding and sleeping on the
tide edge. Tide ebbing. General appearance Black Grey & white but one or two birds were buffish about the upper breast and shoulders.

39

39 Sanderlings, *Calidris alba,* at the tide edge, Lligwy Beach, September 8th, 1948.
40 Adult ruff, *Philomachus pugnax,* in moult. Two views of the same bird, Cob Lake, August 26th, 1952.
41 Curlew sandpipers, *Calidris ferruginea,* with a dunlin, *Calidris alpina,* (right centre) Cob Lake, September 9th, 1952.

Oh Lake. Aug 26
adult Ruff in moult.
Doing much preening

(Two views of the same
bird)

Sept. 9th Bolt Lake.
5 Curlew Sandpipers with one
Dunlin. Dunlin's bill almost
identical in size and curve with C.S's

Ruffs. Sept 2nd to Sept 10th
Malltraeth field pools. 5 was the greatest
numbers seen. Variation in size very apparent
the larger birds appearing more suffused with
warm buff, the smaller more black & white in
the lacing of the scapulars & wings

Will often stand more
erect than this

42

42 Ruffs, *Philomachus pugnax*, at Malltraeth Field pools, September 2nd to 10th, 1945.

43

43 Black-tailed godwit, *Limosa limosa*, feeding, Glan Avon, September 1944.

Stroking its bill and its middle claw.

May 4. York Ferry. Heron perched on side-rail of the ferry causeway.

His white tip not always present in imm. birds seen today

May 4ᵗʰ Mr. Wisart Marsh. Hangasto Immature Lesser Black Backs. Several feeding on pasture in company with adult L.B.B.s and Herring Gulls.

Redshank (First winter Plumage?)
Malltraeth Lake Sept. 15

45

44 Heron, *Ardea cinerea*, at Foel Ferry and immature lesser black-backed gull, *Larus fuscus*, at Malltraeth, May 4th, 1952.
45 Redshank, *Tringa totanus*, Malltraeth Lake, September 15th, 1946.

May 3rd & 4th.
Small flock of Dunlin on Bel Lake. All birds in
bright new plumage, very fresh and clean. A migrating
flock. feeding chiefly deep by the above.

May 3rd & 4th: Common Sandpiper on
shore of Side Lake. 3 birds. One of the birds
was browner in colour than other two and its eye stripe
was pale buff whereas on the other it was white

46

46 Dunlin, *Calidris alpina,* in breeding plumage and common sandpipers, *Tringa hypoleucos,*
Cob Lake, May 3rd and 4th, 1952.

47 Black-tailed godwits, *Limosa limosa,* and a snipe, *Gallinago gallinago,* Field Pools, Bont Farm,
early August, 1948.

March. 27' Cob Lake. 3 Greenshanks about the Lake this morning. Wind blowing feathers up.

48

48 Greenshank, *Tringa nebularia*, at Cob Lake. Wind ruffling feathers. March 27th, 1952.
49 Little stints, *Calidris minuta*, at Cob Lake, September 12th and 13th, 1952.

Little Stints. Bala Lake. Sept. 12 - 13.

Either a pair or a single bird seen at intervals
for some days. When [...] with Dunlin [...]
[...] rise with the flock but
keep on the margin
of it.

[...] shaking

On Sept. 16 this [...] bird
[...] with two others.

50 Studies of purple sandpipers, *Calidris maritima,* at Llandwyn Lighthouse, January 8th, 1950.
51 Bar-tailed godwits, *Limosa lapponica,* at Iona, September 24th, 1934.

Sept. 24ᵗ IONA.   Godwit.   On tide edge feeding with Oyster-catchers.
In small numbers 5 or 6

In size slightly less than Oyster-catchers
which bullies them from their feeding.

52 Pair of curlew, *Numenius arquata*, feeding on rough pasture, Goldsitch Moss, April 14th, 1947.

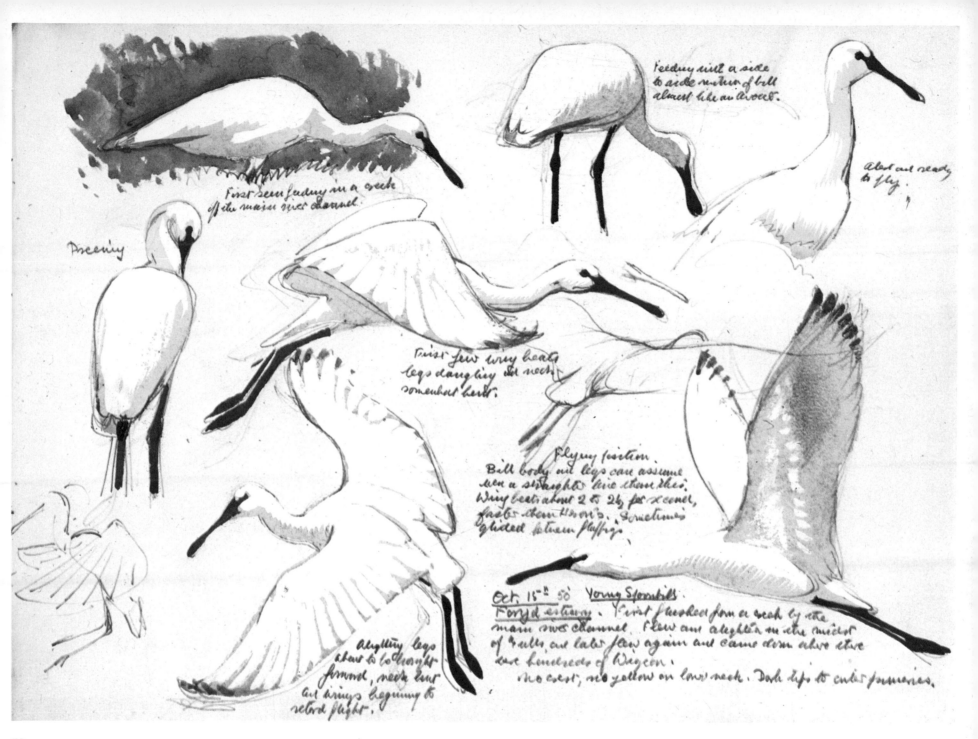

53 Studies of young spoonbill, *Platalea leucorodia*, Foryd estuary, October 15th, 1950.

After swallowing fish its passage could be observed down the neck of the heron

Straining to swallow the fish.

Trying to disgorge it.

Nov 14th. By Shorelands. Heron with flat-fish stuck in its throat. In this state for perhaps ½ hour. Could neither swallow it nor voist it for a time.

Picking it up again after disgorging it.

54

54 Immature heron, *Ardea cinerea,* swallowing a flatfish, Shorelands, November 14th, 1947.

Dark grey centres
pale edges

Dark streaked

pale fawn

Aug 31st. Malltraeth Pool.
Curlew Sandpiper. 3 with a flock
of 20 Dunlin feeding on the mud
of the shallows there in company with
Black tailed Godwit.

55

55 Curlew sandpiper, *Calidris ferruginea,* at Malltraeth Pool, August 31st, 1945.

May 12th London Zoo
Bird in foreground with less contrast of black
and white especially on back and inner secondaries
(More poses in rough note-book)

56

56 Avocets, *Recurvirostra avosetta*, at London Zoo, May 12th, 1949.
57 Lapwings, *Vanellus vanellus*, at Redesmere, March 12th, 1939.

Lapwing. Radcmore. March 12th.
This bird had a black chin and throat
but still had pale edges to the hinder
scapulars.
Feeding on pasture and between its
finds kept patting the ground with its
foot. The leg trembled as it
was raised and brought down
on the flat of the foot.

This bird had a
very mottled throat and
chin and the black on the
chest was also broken
as above. Buffish face
and pale edges to the
hinder scapulars.

58 Bar-tailed godwits, *Limosa lapponica*, threatening, Malltraeth Field Pool, August 2nd, 1948.

Geese, Ducks and Swans

59 Grey lag, *Anser anser*, grazing in a marshy field, January 4th, 1951.

60

60 Barnacle goslings, *Branta leucopsis*, from sketches made at Kendal, July 27th, 1944.

61 Pair of gadwall, *Anas strepera*, Cemlyn Lake, March 15th, 1951.

Oct. 29ᵗ Redesmere. Part of a flock of
32 Canadas resting in the shallows of the
mere. They were not afloat but were standing
on the bottom. Water silvery grey with
subtle darker grey ripples causing the reflections
of geese were tints to become elongated.
Geese were exquisite against the grey background.
Lightest part was the top of the breast which became
a shade of lilac grey below and at the side becoming
pale grey-brown darkening to sepia at the end of flanks.
Backs were a soft brown the pale edges of feathers not
apparent unless one looked for them.

one goose had
a peculiar bunch of
sepia fawn down at
the back of the upper neck

62 Canada geese, *Branta canadensis,* at Redesmere, October 29th, 1944.
63 Grey lag, *Anser anser,* in wing moult, Y Felin, July 12th, 1952.

63

64 Studies of bill markings in Bewick's swans, *Cygnus columbianus*, Malltraeth Lake,
February 24th, 1946.
65 Domestic goose, *Anser domesticus*, August 1942.
66 Flying great crested grebe, *Podiceps cristatus*, and (below) coot chick, *Fulica atra*, Redesmere,
June 9th, 1938.

June 9th
Redshore.

Grebe (Achris) flying.
Legs and feet very conspicuous
trailing behind. Wing beats rapid.

Slow to land.

Bluish scarlet.

"scarlet"
P. Tip.

Ginger down on a darker base.

Pale down.

Young Coot.
June 9th
Redshore.

Where the light is
behind the bird the
beak looks semi-
transparent and the
tip dark (probably
denser at the tip)
but when the light
is on the beak the tip
is pale.

A brood of 4 being fed by
the parent birds on what looked
like young tender, water lily shoots.

66

67 Pintails, *Anas acuta*, at Cob Lake, Easter Monday, March 26th, 1951.

first position when
alarmed →

2nd position
↓

Younger Geese have
not nearly such a
large knob and no
orange showing

Chinese Geese.   Nov. 24

Bradley Hall.
Nr Clitheroe

68

Red breasted Geese. Zoo. May 22nd.

68 Domestic Chinese goose, *Anser cygnoides*, Bradley Hall, near Clitheroe, November 24th, 1934.

69 Red-breasted geese, *Branta ruficollis*, at London Zoo, May 22nd, 1952.

70 Studies of Bewick's swans, *Cygnus columbianus*, taking off and landing, Malltraeth Lake, February 1946.

71 Domestic goose, *Anser domesticus*, August 1942.

Wing stretching.
Sometimes the wing is brought back so that
its inner secondaries are covering tail, rump
and part of the other wing. This side wing is
usually held a little apart from the body whilst
in the stretching position but is not in any way opened

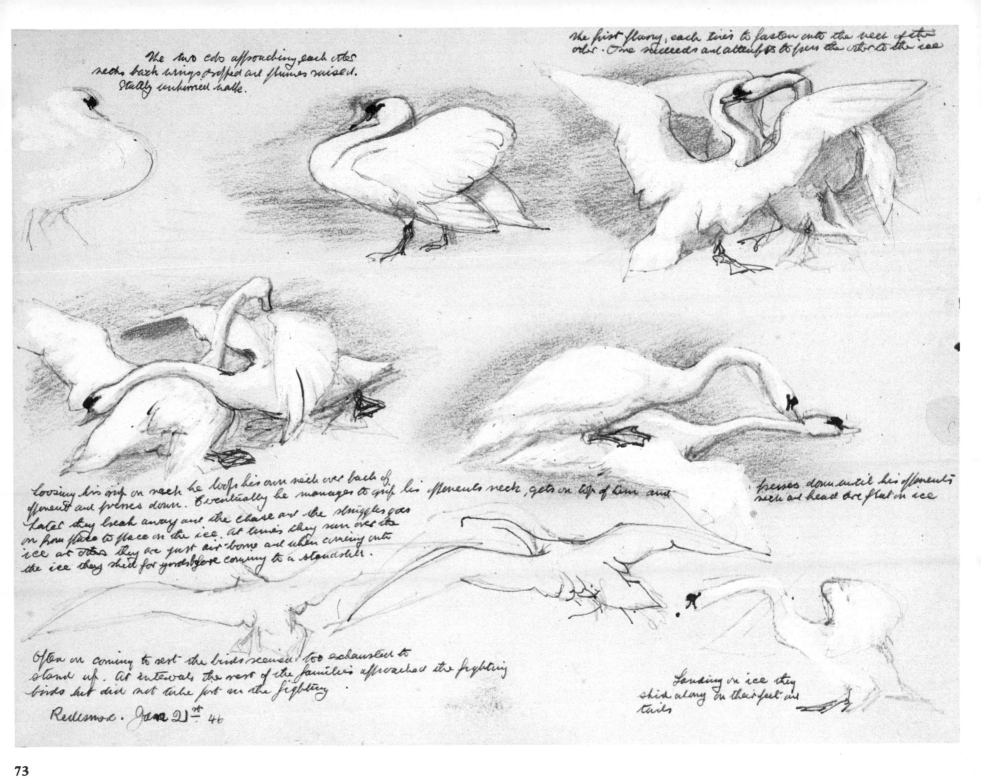

The two cobs approaching each other, necks back wings dropped and plumes raised. Stately unhurried walk.

The first flurry, each tries to fasten onto the neck of the other. One succeeds and attempts to press the other to the ice

Loosing his grip on neck he loops his own neck over back of opponent and presses down. Eventually he manages to grip his opponents neck, gets on top of him and presses down until his opponents neck and head are flat on ice

Later they break away and the chase and the struggles goes on from place to place on the ice. At times they run over the ice at others they are just air-bourne and when coming onto the ice they skid for yards before coming to a standstill.

Often on coming to rest the birds seemed too exhausted to stand up. At intervals the rest of the families approached the fighting birds but did not take part in the fighting

Landing on ice they skid along on their feet and tails

Redesmere. Jan 21st. 46

73

72 Further studies of the domestic goose, including wing-stretching, August 1942.
73 Male swans, *Cygnus olor*, fighting, Redesmere, January 21st, 1946.

74

74 Muscovy ducklings, *Cairina moschata*, Northwich, Cheshire, June 30th, 1947.
75 Mallard drake, *Anas platyrhynchos*, Serpentine, London and (below) pintail drake, *Anas acuta*, at London Zoo, May 11th, 1938.

Mallard. September. Prmy?

Pintail. Zoo

Rest of scapulars very faded,
almost silvery.

shew dark feathers here.

Aug 27ᵗʰ Young Sheld duck one brood
of 18 on Cob Lake.

76 Young shelduck, *Tadorna tadorna*, at Cob Lake, August 8th, 1951.

TY GWYN. May 26th   Shelduck on the Green Marsh.

Shelduck on the marsh in pairs. Often one of the pair would be feeding in the shallow pools while the other would stand by as if on guard. There was some display consisting of head and neck movement. Head and neck alternately stretched vertically and then curved until bill touches the breast or chest.

Frequently flew short distances about the marsh, the pair keeping close.

77 Shelduck, *Tadorna tadorna*, on the Green Marsh, Ty Gwyn, May 26th, 1945.

Sept 8th Malltraeth Marsh. Flock of geese preening and washing. Flapping half closed wings one way throwing water up, often mouth open while doing it.

78 Composition study of the white domestic goose, August, 1942.
79 Domestic geese, *Anser domesticus*, at Malltraeth Marsh, September 8th, 1944.

Shelduck Traeth Bach May 28ᵗʰ

Ducks much duller in colour than drake
This male had a very small knob on bill

SHELDUCK—
LADIE FOWLS. Welsh.

50

80

80 Shelduck, *Tadorna tadorna* (female in foreground), Traeth Bach, May 28th, 1945.

81 Mallard, *Anas platyrhynchos*, at Redesmere, February 9th, 1946.

Birtles Pool . March 5th. Canada fair on the ice and frozen muds Birds in very immaculate plumage . Dead growth behind is - rushes and tall Willow herb.

82 Canada geese, *Branta canadensis,* at Birtles Pool, March 5th, 1946.

Capesthorne Pool, Sept. 8th. Very warm afternoon.
Geese sleepy and rested with heads back.
Bright sunlight. Geese in reflection of yellow, brown
and green reeds. Slight ripple on the water. Fresh
green of lily-leaves (yellow lily) Some reared out of
the water. Geese very sepia in colour.

83 Canada geese, *Branta canadensis*, resting at Capesthorne Pool, September 8th, 1942.
84 Studies of the great crested grebe, *Podiceps eristatus*, and young, Redesmere, July 1935.
85 Drake mallard, *Anas platyrhynchos*, sequence of moult, Gawsworth Pool, July/August 1935.

Mallard Drake in
eclipse P.   July 1st.
Both these stages seen on the same
day.

Gaunsworth
Pool.

July 1st

Later stage of moult

(2)

Fairly early stage of moult

July 1st
(1)

Had the beginnings of the white
ring on neck as a thin line
round the front of the neck.
(not seen in this posit.)

Aug 18th

(3)   Aug 4th

Lower Breast of this bird a pearly grey with
indefinite finely brown, crescentic markings on the outer sides.
(4)   Aug 4th

85

86 Juvenile shelduck, *Tadorna tadorna*, at Cob Lake, August 27th, 1949.

87 Family of Bewick's swans, *Cygnus columbianus*, Malltraeth Lake, February 20th, 1946.

Barnacle family at Mr Abbott's, Sawmill Lane,
Kendal.
From drawings made July 27th.
Goslings Hatched July 14th. nest made on the edge of
a quarry cliff. Parent birds are birds which were winged
by Mr Abbott on wild-fowling expeditions.

88 Barnacle geese, *Branta leucopsis*, and goslings, Kendal, July 1944.

Feb 15th. Llyn Coron.

Water swarming with duck, chiefly Wigeon, with Shoveller
Teal, Tufted, Pochard. Big majority Wigeon the drakes whistling
so that the place was full of their calls. One excited group of
one duck and five drakes sped across the water this way and
that and when the duck came down to the surface other
drakes joined the group and at one time she was chased
by eight or nine drakes.

Sometimes the duck would
suddenly change direction and seemed
to cut through the group of pursuing
drakes.

Sweeping up in a
glide

attitude when swimming
about calling. The drake
seemed to display a larger [?] bit
of white on wing than normal

occasionally this attitude
was adopted by a drake when the
company alighted

89 Wigeon, *Anas penelope*, at Llyn Coron, February 15th, 1951.

89

July 6th. Redesmere.

Moorhen with young among water lilies
She with wings much crooked and held
thigh. Fed the young with bits from the flowers
and also from living things from the leaves

90 Moorhen, *Gallinula chloropus*, with chick, Redesmere, July 6th, 1945.

Birds of Prey

Aug 13th. Shorelands.
Juvenile Little Owl.
Brought in a paper bag
by two boys from Capel Manor.
Could not fly when it came to
us. Fed on rabbit and dead
birds. Aug 15th strong on the
wing and very fit

Pose adopted when ready to fly off perch.
Often with a bobbing up and down of head and neck.

91 Studies of a juvenile little owl, *Athene noctua,* hand-reared by the artist, Shorelands,
August 13th, 1951.

92

92 Snowy owl, *Nyctea scandiaca,* at Chester Zoo, January 29th–February 9th, 1946.

93 Snowy owl, *Nyctea scandiaca,* at Chester Zoo, possibly a young male, January 29th, 1946.

94 Gyr falcon, *Falco rusticolus,* owned by Ronald Stevens, August 1951.

95 Female sparrowhawk, *Accipiter nisus,* on the garden wall, Shorelands, September 1st, 1949.

Jan 29th Snowy owl at Chester Zoo.
this owl not as large as some
specimens seen and may ~~not have~~
~~been~~ be a young male (first winter)

Gyr Falcon owned by Ronald Stevens
Mid August.

Sept 1st Evening
Sparrow Hawk on the
garden wall. Rested
for some minutes on the wall
near the kitchen door. No
other birds to be seen.
N.B. Flights were held at the
sides of the tail not
above it.

Falcon
South Stack.
July 6ᵗʰ

96 Peregrine falcon, *Falco peregrinus*, South Stack, Holy Island, July, probably 1948.

Falcon resting on cliff. Her back feathers beginning to look bleached and a little dowdy.

"Tough guy" pose of falcon just after alighting.

Tiercel perched on a clump of samphire growing from the sheer face of the cliff. He rested here for at least two hours during the morning of July 12ᵗʰ.

July 12ᵗʰ

Falcon cleaning her bill. Cleans each side alternately with a side to side motion of her head.

97 Peregrines, *Falco peregrinus*, at South Stack; the tiercel (left) and falcon, July, probably 1948.

June 30th
Falcon feeding eyasses
One much more advanced
in fledging than the
other

98 Female ('falcon') peregrine, *Falco peregrinus*, with eyasses, South Stack. June 30th, probably 1948.
99 Study of Ken Williams' Turumti (red-headed) falcon, *Falco chiquera*, c. 1962.
100 & 101 Young sparrowhawks, *Accipiter nisus*, at Hawks-head Clough, July 15th, 1947.
102 Study of a barn owl, *Tyto alba*, autumn 1934.

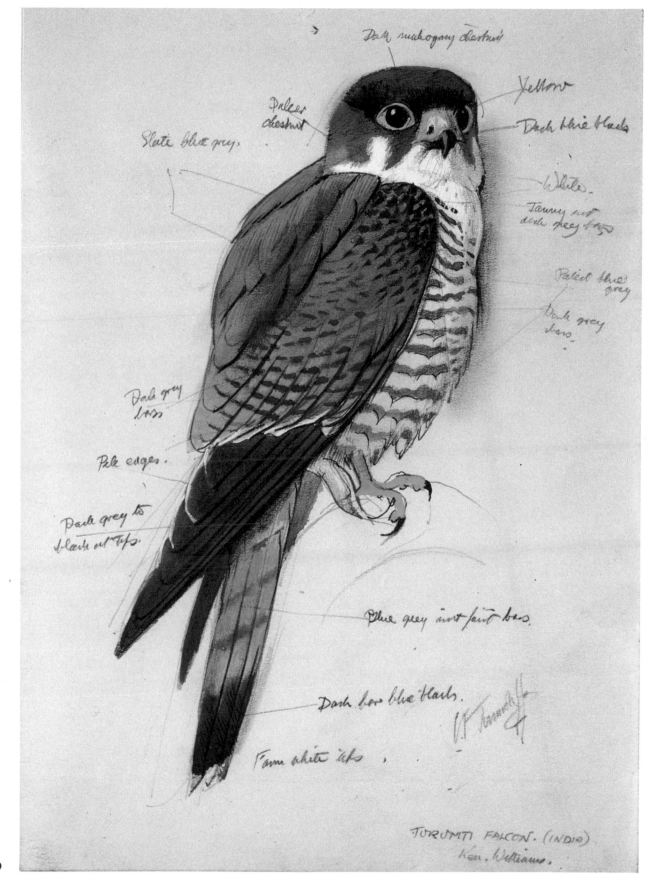

Dark mahogany chestnut

Paler chestnut

Slate blue grey.

Yellow

Dark blue black

White.

Tawny not dark grey bars

Paler blue grey

Dark grey bars.

Dark grey bars

Pale edges.

Dark grey to black at tips.

Blue grey not faint bars.

Dark bow blue black.

Faint white tips.

TURUMTI FALCON. (INDIA)

Ken. Williams.

Impression from memory of the cock bird which alighted on nest for an instant.

the side of the silvery white 2 dark bars sh...

Under tail a silver grey with two conspicuous dark bars.

July 15th Hawks-head Clough

July 15

Miscellaneous Birds

The Ring Plover often nestles
in a hollow of the weed so
that their legs were hidden.

The group was more spread out
and not so evenly placed as here.
Turnstones were throwing the seaweed over.

Sept. 7th.
Dinas Point.

Ring Plover and Turnstones.
Some young birds among the
R. Plover. Legs of young much
paler than adult, chest mark brown
and not complete. No black above the
eye.

103 Group of adult and immature ringed plovers, *Charadrius hiaticula*, with turnstones,
Arenaria interpres, behind, Dinas Point, September 7th, 1944.

104 An early wheatear, *Oenanthe oenanthe*, at Shorelands, and wrens, *Troglodytes troglodytes*, at Crochan Caffo, April, 1951.

105 Singing wren, *Troglodytes troglodytes*, wren collecting nesting material and (below) wood warbler, *Phylloscopus sibilatrix*, and willow warbler, *Phylloscopus trochilus*, May 13th, 1947.

May. 13ᵉ Wren at
Dovebridge. Song on a
stump.

Carrying nest material.
Sang a few loud bars while still
carrying this green moss in its beak.

Bill seemed to be
held rather more lifted up than
with Willow W.

Wood Warbler.

Willow Warbler.
This bird came to
her nest, situated
in a futile of bracken
close to ground, while we
sat only five feet away.
Veggo our nest.

105

106 A cock green woodpecker, *Picus viridis,* with two juveniles at Shorelands, July 25th, 1951.
107 Female great spotted woodpecker, *Dendrocopos major,* Chester Zoo, August 3rd, 1939.
108 Young jay, *Garrulus glandarius,* study from a dead bird, July 6th and 7th, 1934.
109 Notes from a day at South Stack, March 10th, 1952.

Iris in juvenile
appear dull brown
and in most lights
the eye appears dark.

Shoelands. July 25th

An adult cock and
two young Green Woodpeckers perched on the shoe wall, 8 to 9 am.
Later all flew down to concrete paving and began to feed
in the cracks between the flat stones.
Adult called intermittently as if to keep the young near to.
A high-pitched clear note repeated about 3 times per second.
Call of juveniles rather reedy and throaty, not quite so high as adult.

adult wing
stretching

♀ "Greater Spotted Woodpecker.
Chester Zoo. Aug 3rd.

Cheadle Mark

Blue Grey

Red

When perched on upright
trunk the wings are carried
close onto its tail. Back and tail
a continuous line

Wing
has a

Young Jay. (from dead bird) July 6th ♂
Blue feathers on the wing not so definately
marked with black & white as in adult bird.
Also head neck and back browner
Length when stretched out about 12"

March 10th. Soth Stack. From the lighthouse steps, and looking through the hole in the rock, saw two fulmars resting on the ledges and also saw another flying about the cliff. Near them a group of Guillemots (8) also noted on the ledges, and in the same vicinity a few groups of 2 and 3 Guillemots. While we watched they all left the cliff as if alarmed at our scouting. Razorbills were seen flying about the cliffs and over the water but none rested on the cliffs.

Late a Peregrine flew out from the cliff beyond Helen's calling
Tower and as we climbed the steps a pair of Ravens flew about the cliffs. In a triangular niche in the cliff was a pile of twist material and I thought I detected new material in the cup (this the site of a previous Raven's nest.)

All the previous year's guano had been washed from the cliff.

There were about 30 Guillemots on the ledges when we arrived.

Herring Gulls were dotted about the cliff in pairs as if they had already staked out their claim for nesting sites

Later we climbed the steps and went down the headlands by Helen's Tower
On the way down watched a cork Stonechat singing on a rock. He he rang be moved his tail up and down, and his throat swelled as he sang.

A gorse was coming into flower, saw a fine well out though in its seaward side it was very brown as if it had been burnt — the results of salt-laden gales I suspect.
Looking from the cliff edge down to the sea we saw a solitary Shag swimming.
In previous years a solitary pair had nested near the foot of these cliffs
Moving along the cliff such a Peregrine again went out from the cliff calling loudly. It flew about and glided for a time then turned up the headland and disappeared off over the skyline.

Near the place where the great cliffs jut out almost at right angles to the general line a pair of Ravens left the cliff and flew about suspiciously but we could find no sign of a nest: Later they returned and flew round again but we still failed to find a nest or sign of one.
When we returned to Helen's Tower a Peregrine flew out from the cliff opposite, again calling, and after circling swung over the sea and the lighthouse came into the cliff again but then turned out of sight in the cliff opposite the steps. While in flight it was several times mobbed by herring gulls but easily eluded them.

Sept. 19. Adult and young
Goldfinch on the shore wall, Shorelands.
Young asking for food, wings extended
and quivering. Adult regurgitates a
white jelly-like shape into the bill
and spasmodically jabs this into the
open bill of young. On the wall,
near the Goldfinches, were House-Sparrows,
curious and aggressive. While feeding
was taking place a sparrow approached
and hustled the Goldfinches off the
wall, tweaking the tail of the
finch just before it flew.
Adult Goldfinch seemed
in moult. Body feathers
loose and rather untidy.

110 Goldfinch, *Carduelis carduelis*, feeding young at Shorelands, September 19th, 1949.

III Hoopoe, *Upupa epops*, at Shorelands, October 1951.

Aug. 14ᵗʰ Clough Brook, Wildboarclough.
Cock Grey Wagtail in moult.
Outer tail feathers half-grown.
Remains of black throat still visible.
Some inner secondaries missing.

When preening, dropped wings
so that lower back and rump
were visible.

112

112 Cock grey wagtail, *Motacilla cinerea,* in moult, Clough Brook, August 14th, 1944.
113 Juvenile long-tailed tit, *Aegithalos caudatus,* Radnor Mere, June 26th, 1939.

Looks very
plump when at ease

Wheatears on the dried-up bed of
Barley Reservoir feeding on worms. April 28th.

June 9th Cob Lake Shore.

Feeding

115

114 Studies of a cock wheatear, *Oenanthe oenanthe*, Bosley Reservoir, April 28th, 1938.
115 A ruff, *Philomachus pugnax*, in breeding plumage, Cob Lake, June 9th, 1949.

116 Cuckoo, *Cuculus canorus,* on barbed wire, April 1946.

March 13th Redesmere.
Small company of Redpolls - 6 or 7 birds.
feeding on the alders at the side of
mere. Sometimes they dropped to the
ground and searched among dead leaves
and plants and grasses.   Day of cold wind

One hen observed was a very
grey bird with very pronounced
light wing bars.

117 Redpolls, *Acanthis flammea,* on an alder branch, Redesmere, March 13th, 1946.

In an ash at Alderley Edge.
Aug. 22nd   "Greenfinch feeding young.
Young are constantly calling and flapping half-open
wings. Food is thrust into the bill of young
by parent who seems to regurgitate as no food
was visible in her bill before she fed the young.

118

118 Greenfinch, *Carduelis chloris*, feeding young, Alderley Edge, August 22nd, 1944.
119 Spotted flycatcher, *Muscicapa striata*, with young, Gawsworth, July 11th, 1944.

April 6th. Radnor Woods. Gt. Sp. Woodpecker.

120

120 Great spotted woodpecker, *Dendrocopos major*, Radnor Woods, April 6th, 1947.
121 Cock chaffinch, *Fringilla coelebs*, at Redesmere, March 9th, 1939.

Pont Abat Glaslyn. May 1st 1952. Two ♂ and one ♀
Pied Flycatcher seen near the bridge. One male flew
to a hole in an oak, the entrance to last year's nest
of Pied Flycatchers. It is clear that the pair intend
to use this same site. Several times the other male
was chased away by the paired male.

122 Two male pied flycatchers, *Muscicapa hypoleuca*, and a female, Pont Aber Glâslyn, May 1st, 1952.
123 Studies of pied flycatchers, *Muscicapa hypoleuca*, at Pont Aber Glaslyn, April 22nd, 1951.

Books of Ornithological Interest Illustrated by C.F. Tunnicliffe

BAYNE, Charles S., *Call of the Birds*, with illustrations by C. F. Tunnicliffe. Revised edition. London, Collins, 1945. 10 full page, 18 text black and white illustrations.

BENNETT, Linda, *RSPB Book of Garden Birds*, with 36 plates in colour by C. F. Tunnicliffe, R.A., and line drawings by Robert Gillmor. London, Hamlyn, 1978.

DAY, J. Wentworth, *British Birds of the Wild Places*, London, Blandford Press, 1961. 49 colour and 19 black and white illustrations.

JEFFERIES, Richard, *Wild Life in a Southern County*, with an introduction and notes by Samuel J. Looker. Wood engravings by C. F. Tunnicliffe. London, Lutterworth Press, 1949. 21 wood engravings (13 of birds).

LOCKLEY, R. M., *Letters from Skokholm*, London, Dent, 1947. 52 illustrations.

PRIESTLEY, Mary (Editor), *A Book of Birds*, London, Gollancz, 1937. 82 wood engravings.

ROGERSON, Sidney and TUNNICLIFFE, Charles Frederick, *Our Bird Book*, London, Collins, 1947. 52 colour and 84 black and white illustrations.

TUNNICLIFFE, C. F., *Bird Portraiture*, London, The Studio, 1945. 16 colour plates and 87 monochrome illustrations.

TUNNICLIFFE, C. F., *Birds of the Estuary*, Harmondsworth, Penguin Books, 1952. 16 colour and 16 black and white illustrations.

TUNNICLIFFE, C. F., *Mereside Chronicle*, London, Country Life, 1948. Numerous monochrome illustrations.

TUNNICLIFFE, C. F., *My Country Book*, London, The Studio, 1942. 16 colour plates (6 of birds) and 81 monochrome (37 of birds).

TUNNICLIFFE, C. F., *Shorelands Summer Diary*, London, Collins, 1952. 16 colour plates (all of birds) and numerous black and white (many of birds).

VESEY-FITZGERALD, Brian, *Rivermouth*, London, Eyre and Spottiswoode, 1949. 6 full page and 7 text black and white illustrations (many of birds).

WILLIAMSON, Henry, *The Lone Swallows, and Other Essays of Boyhood and Youth*, London, Putnam, 1933. 23 full page and 34 text wood engravings (some of birds).

WILLIAMSON, Henry, *The Peregrine's Saga, and Other Wild Tales*, London, Putnam, 1934. 23 full page and 12 text wood engravings (some of birds).

WILLIAMSON, Kenneth, *The Sky's Their Highway*, London, Putnam, 1937. 8 wood engravings.

compiled by Keith Cheyney